BUILDER
TO
PROPERTY
INVESTOR

ISBN - Paperback: 9798679978126

Credits:

SIMON ZUTSHI (Crowd property, property investors network, Property Magic) mentor

ANDY HAYNES (property here, property investors network) coach

SANJAY SHAH, DAVE HOLLOWAY (emotional mastery) coach

Everyone on (Mastermind 28) property group support

FOTEINI, MIA, and LEON (my family) wife, daughter, and son

BUILDER TO PROPERTY INVESTOR

My story and how to start investing in property with little or no money while creating a passive income

SEBASTIAN MACFARLANE

DISCLAIMER

The information in this book is for educational purposes only. The contents do not constitute financial advice in any way, and you should seek independent professional advice before making any investment. Investing in property can be risky, just like any other investment. Historical growth in property prices does not necessarily mean that prices will increase in the future. Your property may be repossessed if you do not keep up repayments on your mortgage.

The information presented herein represents the view of the author as of the date of publication. Because of the rate at which conditions change, the author reserves the right to alter and update his opinion based on new conditions. This is for informational purposes only. While every attempt has been made to verify the information provided, the author does not assume any responsibility for errors, inaccuracies, or omissions.

Sebastian Macfarlane/Propertyfix Investors Ltd. is/are not licensed or regulated by the Financial Conduct Authority and does not provide financial advice. Do not invest unless you have carefully thought about whether you can afford to and whether it is right for you. We strongly recommend that you seek appropriate professional advice before entering into any contract. This investment is not regulated by the Financial Conduct Authority or covered by the Financial Service Compensation Scheme or the Financial Ombudsman Service.

Contents

WHAT PEOPLE SAY ABOUT ME

Simon Zutshi (founder of CrowdProperty and property investors network)

Sebastian is an exceptional young man with a can-do attitude. The go-to guy for development projects and extremely knowledgeable in property investing, he has the complete package when it comes to property, as he has the building experience combined with up-to-date knowledge on the latest investment strategies. Highly recommended.

Jennifer Lin (property investor)

It gives me great pleasure to strongly recommend Sebastian and Foteini Araka Macfarlane. Seb and Foteini and I met in 2019 at Simon Zutshi's Mastermind course, learning together advanced property investment strategies, during which I was most impressed by their dedication to learning to add to their already abundant combined developers' knowledge. I subsequently gave a private investment for their HMO project in Norwich. Over the course of the project, they not only kept excellent communication, providing regular updates throughout the project, but also completed the project with the highest standards and professionalism. They are both easy to work with, trustworthy, and always ready to help, no matter how busy they are. Seb and Foteini stand out for their commitment, perseverance, and teamwork, and I'm completely confident that they will surpass all expectations in their property journey!

Annette Deguara (property investor)

It's been great working with Seb and Foteini. I invested some funds with them on a short-term basis for their HMO project in Norwich. The terms of the loan were set out clearly from the outset. During the course of the investment, they kept me updated regularly on the progress of the project. In fact, I had my funds returned earlier than expected! They've done an amazing job on the property, and I'd be more than happy to invest with them again in the future.

ACRONYMS

BTL	Buy-to-let
HMOs	Houses in multiple occupation
BRRR	Buy, refurbish, refinance, and rent
BMV	Below market value
R2R	Rent-to-rent
SA	Serviced accommodation
PLO	Purchase lease option
PO	Purchase option
EDC	Exchange with delayed completion
SPV	Special purchase vehicle
LTV	Loan to value
LGDV	Loan to gross development value
GDV	Gross development value
JV	Joint venture
POC	Profit on cost
ROI	Return on investment
ROE	Return on equity

You don't know what you don't know!

Most people think property investing is saving up for a deposit, buying a house, doing it up, and flogging it at a profit. But what if I told you there is another way? A smarter way, a way that you can start with little or no money, and not only that, a way that will give you a passive income too, achievable within very little time?

If you are reading this book, then, like me, you are looking for answers in the form of knowledge, so I congratulate you for getting this far; it means you are already taking action! I am a firm believer in education to better yourself, and this book tells my story to help illustrate what's possible if you put your mind to something. It will show you how you can start property investing with little or no money, and, after reading it, you will already know more than most property investors.

My aim with this book is to give you the tools – knowledge, information, and mindset – to get started in, and succeed in, property investing. And I have also spent some time talking about my story and my experiences. This is because I believe it is important to understand that this is something you can achieve starting with very little – as I did. You don't need to have money to invest (though of course, that makes things easier). But it's also important to understand the level of commitment and belief in yourself necessary to make that happen. I hope you can learn from me and this book and enjoy the journey!

CHAPTER 1

HOW I GOT INTO PROPERTY INVESTING

I'm not your typical high-flying investor type. In fact, nothing could have been further from my mind when I started my journey. I'd like to tell my story, briefly, so you can see that I'm not unique here: this path is open to anyone – to you. You just have to have the desire and the drive to make it happen. And I hope that with this book at your side, your journey will be much easier than mine!

BUILDER

It all started when I was 17 years old and had a job restoring furniture in a small Suffolk village. I had just left school, when I got a job as an antique restorer at one of the many antique shops in town. While working there, I met a fellow antique dealer on the same street where I worked, who was also a local builder/carpenter. He approached me and my carpentry skills to help on a barn conversion he was doing for himself. At the time, I was on minimum wage, and he offered me a much better rate that seemed like megabucks to me, so I jumped at the chance.

While working with him every week, I would buy a new tool with my wages, building up a toolkit of my own and learning all about building and renovating properties. Working with him nurtured my love for property and renovating it. Building requires creative thinking and constant problem solving; this came naturally to me, and it turned out I was pretty good at it too. I learned a lot while working with him, and I will always thank him for inspiring me.

Over the next five years or so, I continued to develop my portfolio of building and refurbishment skills, working for a variety of builders both in the UK and overseas, and then, in 2008, I decided to start my own "odd-jobbing" business, along with my soon-to-be wife.

I would literally take on any building job, and the jobs were now steadily getting bigger and bigger, up to then being asked to take on a complete barn conversion by a friend. I am a "yes man", and I would just say yes to literally any job, no matter how big or difficult it was, and find a way to make it happen. If I didn't know something, I would just find someone who did to help me and learn from them for the next time. I worked to learn and for the love of it. It was great; I was getting paid for a hobby that I had all the enthusiasm in the world for.

My first turning point came in 2011 with the arrival of my daughter and marriage to my wife. That was it! I needed to start taking work more seriously to be able to provide for my new family properly, so in 2011 I formed Propertyfix Builders Ltd. This meant acquiring a whole new set of skills. I taught myself to create a website, rented an office with a lock-up as a base for the company and to house all the tools and equipment that I had accumulated over the years, and began to take on staff.

Each job was teaching me something new, and as I was growing, I was constantly learning new things. Things like industry standard building regulations, acquisition of planning permission, building from structural engineers' drawings, reading architects' plans, JCT contracts, dealing with staff and customers, running a limited company, and so on. These have become second nature to me now.

For me, business is all about imagination and relation-ships, and, in between, people skills, good communication, enthusiasm, and a positive "can-do" attitude, while continuing to learn and adapt.

The next thing was to buy a house for my new family. At the time, we were renting a three-bed new-build, where we had been settled for a few years. I knew that I needed to stop renting and get a mortgage, as It was obvious to me that to get a mortgage for a fixed amount of money on a property that would be continuously rising in value was a sound investment. We had the chance to buy the house we were renting, but the challenge now was that I didn't have the deposit money needed to even get a mortgage to buy the house. That didn't matter, though, as I was so determined to find a way. I knew that it would work out. I quickly set to asking all the banks for a loan and everyone I knew for help too. After a month or so of asking around, I eventually managed to get someone to get a bank loan for me for the 5% deposit, to then get the £225k mortgage needed to buy the house. This really was a testament to a "can do" attitude and that perseverance will always prevail. I had made it happen. I strongly believe that if you think you can, you can, and if you think you can't, you can't. And that thoughts really do become things by making a decision and taking action on that decision.

Then my life fell apart.

Within a month, I learned that my best friend was terminally ill, and, in the stress of dealing with this, I lost my driving licence. These two events combined were to have a devastating effect on my mental health and in turn on my building company.

The party was over.I became massively depressed, and it wasn't long before I didn't even want to leave the house. My now "can't-do" negative attitude, combined with having to rely on people for transport, meant my business was suffering badly as a result. Productivity was down, debts were stacking up, and I was struggling to keep up with my monthly payments. My enthusiasm had completely gone, and I felt like there was no future. I was living off the deposits from the following jobs to cover my current outgoings, never managing to catch up. It seemed futile, and I wasn't dealing at all well with all the stress of managing the now sizable 100k-200k refurbs/extensions I was taking on, which previously I had taken within my stride.

I was no longer going to work out of enjoyment but out

of resentment instead. I felt like a slave chained to work with no escape, and that the life I had built was an unsustainable burden around my neck. I desperately needed to find a solution.

EDUCATION

My dad taught me the value of money and my mum always used to say to me, "work smarter, not harder".

I started looking for a solution through reading. I was the kind of guy that (up until then) unless it was a manual or a set of instructions, would never pick up a book, but I was desperate to find a solution. Enough was enough, and it was time to get smart. Everything I had learned until now was enough to get me to where I was, but to move further forward I would need to step it up big time, start reading, and work smarter.

That's when I came across a book by Robert Kiyosaki called "Rich dad, Poor dad". That was a major turning point for me and my understanding of money and how to accumulate wealth. In his book, he explains how the rich think and, more importantly, how to make your money work for you and not work for it, through financial literacy and investing. This was exactly what I had been missing all this time, and it was the key for me to move forward; it was a stake in the ground, giving me rekindled hope of a brand new future.

Through reading his book, I had finally realized that no one was going to help me but me! I needed to face my demons head-on and work double-time if I ever stood a chance of being happy again and able to support the life that I had built.

It was now so blatantly obvious to me that the life basics I had learned at school were a load of rubbish. I would need to set out to find new teachers to learn from, who had their finances in order. People who didn't have to work for money but instead worked for a higher sense of purpose; financially independent people.

After reading that first book, I was hooked in my search for answers, and with my brand new way of thinking I couldn't get enough. So, I kept going and proceeded to read avidly (I've made a reading list for you in the appendix at the end). The more I read, the more I started to notice that they were all saying very similar things and patterns were starting to emerge. It all pointed me in the direction of property investing being my logical progression and solution to my problems. I was also starting to realize that education alone was not getting me to where I wanted to be.

INVEST IN YOURSELF

I needed to step up and make a big commitment to myself and invest in myself first, but how? By now I had accumulated nearly £70k of debt as a result of the previous year's events and had minus zero to invest, so to eliminate distractions and raise the funds that I needed for more education, I decided to temporarily give up my much-loved hobby of motocross enduro. I sold my bike with all the kit, and the very next day invested all the proceeds of around £6K into property training classes. By this time, and after supporting me through the previous year, my amazing wife was starting to get interested in what I was doing too, and it wasn't long until I had her fully on board with me, reading and attending classes together, etc. I was extremely lucky to have had her full support throughout everything I had been through, and to now have her collaborating on my new journey too was incredible, and it brought us closer than ever before.

Then, while at a class together, we heard about a 12-month property mastermind programme that had a hefty price tag of about £30k. It was instantly clear to me how much value this could bring to the table in terms of commitment and investing in yourself, especially with a price tag like that. But being me and on minus zero, it just seemed out of the realms of possibility and a pipe dream. Then, to my disbelief, my wife proceeded to tell me how she had requested a meeting with the organisers for later that day to see if there was any way she and I could sign up for the programme. Armed only with our wits, we went to the meeting and proceeded to tell our story that had led us up to that point of being there. I knew that with my background in the building industry and the fact I had given up my hobby to raise funds to be there showed great commitment. After half an hour of talking, and with this back story, we reached an agreement with the organisers. This now gave me a huge commitment and investment in myself and put me in total debt to the tune of just over £100k, creating a massive incentive to succeed, and I literally couldn't have been more laser-focused. I felt like I had finally turned a corner and had a fantastic opportunity ahead of me. If I did this right, I would not only be able to clear my debts and support my family again with the lifestyle I had built, but if I excelled I would be able to choose if, and when, I wanted to work, which meant I could spend more time with my family plus buy as many motorbikes to go on adventures as I wanted in a couple of years' time if I kept my head down.

I was now fully focused on property investing and needed to learn how to start acquiring investment properties of my own. I knew that I could add value by doing them up and make a profit and already had my building company in place to do just this, but how was I going to get the initial seed capital to fund deposits and get started? I had just added to a debt that I was already in up to my eyeballs and needed to be able to provide for my family as well, and there was no way I was going to fail them! How did other investors raise funds?

"How can I afford it?"

Saying "how?" makes you look for a solution. Saying "I can't afford it" makes you give up.

OTHER PEOPLES MONEY FOR DEPOSITS

It had come to my attention while studying that all professional investors run out of capital to invest at some point and have to find creative ways to raise more funds for deposits; so, the question was, how did they get over this stumbling block?

I started to learn that the answer is by creating an opportunity and bringing value to it while being able to demonstrate potential opportunities to people indirectly. The question to be asking is "who do you know?" The key is to tell absolutely everyone about your opportunity, burn all bridges and go all out; you never know who might have money hidden away in your social circles, as people who have money don't generally go around shouting about it; so, never assume anything.

It's also important that you know what you are doing, and that you do actually bring value to an opportunity, making clear any risks involved, as there are risks with any private money lending; and, if you do use other people's money as a way to fund your deposits, it is extremely important that you are careful and make sure that you can return their money at the agreed time, and that you have a contract drawn up and signed by both parties. More importantly than that, your offer to them must actually be beneficial and give them a better return than they are currently getting in the bank or wherever it is, and on terms that work for them to be a win–win scenario.

Now that I had learnt and understood this, the next thing I needed to do was to start meeting lots of new people and "growing my network". It's a numbers game, so the more people you meet and tell, the more likely you are to meet somebody who you get on with to work with. I started attending networking events alongside the study classes that I was attending and begun growing my network.

NETWORKING

"Your network is your net worth."

I went all-out on networking in a big way. Networking enabled me to start meeting lots and lots of new like-minded people, the kind of people that were in line with my new way of thinking and excited about property too. I would go to every local business and property networking event in my area, along with events all over the UK too. I was living and breathing networking events. The great thing about networking is that there are all sorts of different people out there, who all bring something completely different to the table. This works really well, as everybody can help each other with the skill or resource that the other lacks. For example, I had lots of experience in building/developing and adding value to property but didn't have any capital. Whereas there were other people I met that had no experience in building/developing but lots of capital they wanted to invest in property.

This is why networking is an exceptional tool and an essential part of growing any business.

While networking, I found that most people who are educated in property investing and the return on investment that property could yield were the kind of people that would want a much higher % to work with you, as opposed to Joe public, people who just had savings, business owners, or people with inheritance, who were happier with smaller returns. So long as you beat the banks, they were happy.

* * *

So now you know my story. Let's help you start yours! First, I'm going to look at why it makes so much sense to invest in property.

CHAPTER 2

WHY INVEST IN PROPERTY?

This part of the book looks in detail at property investing and explains the economics of it, how it works, and how profitable it can be. This chapter will help you understand how money in any property will always way outperform any traditional bank, paying you a much better return. There is a good book by Samuel Leads called "Buy low, rent high" that talks about this, which I recommend.

WHEN TO BUY PROPERTY

"Don't wait to buy property – buy property and wait."

The answer is that NOW is always the best time to invest

in property. To understand what will happen in the future with the property market and the best time to buy, you just need to look back at history.

House price fluctuation

If you look back at history, there has always been expansion, followed by recession, followed by expansion, followed by recession. This is evident right through economic history, and this cycle is set to continue into the foreseeable future. In 2008, there was a sizable recession that lasted around six years. In this period, house prices stagnated, and rents haven't moved much for the last 15 years or so. This indicates that it's extremely likely that at some point by 2027 house prices will rise massively, along with rents going up too.

The best time to invest is always during or just after a recession, like right now. With all the uncertainty of Brexit and COVID-19 in the UK of late, this is a prime example of a very good time to buy; some experts are saying 2021 could be the opportunity of the decade!

Great opportunities are often disguised by temporary defeat, failure, or disaster.

When there is a sustained period of uncertainty, just like with Brexit followed by COVID-19, it creates fear.

This fear removes many amateur investors/buyers from the property market, along with many landlords who will want to retire early and sell up from fear of not being able to find tenants, non-paying tenants, and property devaluing.

Combine this with the Section 24 tax change of late for landlords, and this brings lots of property stock to the market at lower prices, along with motivated sellers, repossessions, and fewer buyers frozen by fear to buy them as a result of an anticipated drop in property prices.

During these times, I believe the basic strategy of buying a fixer-upper, doing it up, and flogging it at a profit as a quick flip is a risky one, because with an anticipated drop in property prices you may come unstuck when it's time to sell unless you know how to add a considerable amount of value to a property.

This is all good news for the experienced investor who knows how to acquire property in creative ways, with strategies such as purchase lease options and momentum investing. An investor who looks for motivated vendors, as opposed to a property itself, for more leverage to buy at competitive prices. An investor who knows how to add real value, for example, converting commercial premises to a multi-let residential unit, then refinancing and pulling their money out to be recycled onto the next project, while holding that property for the market to recover.

People generally find excuses not to do something until after an opportunity has passed them by, and then it is too late.

Property prices, on average, double around every ten years or so. This has been the case right through history, and you don't have to look very hard to see that this is the case. That's why the saying goes, "Don't wait to buy property – buy property and wait."

MONEY DEPRECIATES

Leaving your money in a bank over time will depreciate its value. Banks are designed to make money for themselves and not for you. Let me illustrate this.

For example, if you worked really, really hard for a year or two and managed to save up £25k, and then put that money in the bank to have some savings to fall back on, and you left it in there for ten years or so, the interest the banks would give you is so low that after ten years the same £25k you put in there expecting to make some interest and be worth more, would actually be worth less. It would probably be worth around £17k, instead of £25k. This is a result of interest rates always being lower than inflation (adjusted by governments).

The price of living goes up and up, it inflates, while the value of money goes down, it depreciates; so, instead of going up in value it would have actually gone down, it would have depreciated over time.

Money and the gold standard

The gold standard is a monetary system in which a country's currency or paper money is freely convertible into a fixed amount of gold. In other words, physical gold backs the value of money.

The good thing about a gold standard is that it arrests control of the issuance of money out of the hands of governments, with the physical quantity of gold acting as a limit to that issuance.

The gold standard is not currently used by any government. Britain stopped using the gold standard in 1931, and the US followed suit in 1933 and completely abandoned the remnants of the system in 1973.

The moment money was taken off the gold standard, it became fake money. This is because, rather than be tied to physical gold, it became a huge IOU.

When a currency is not tied to gold (a physical asset), governments can print more and more money out of thin air or add some zeros and ones to a computer at the treasury or reserve. This leads to inflation and the devaluing of the purchasing power of that currency.

This is nothing new. Countries from ancient Rome to the Weimar Republic of Germany to modern-day Zimbabwe have printed or debased money to the point of no return. This results in hyperinflation, where money literally becomes worthless.

PROPERTY APPRECIATES

Using the previous sum of £25k that you had saved up, instead of putting it into a bank, this time you invest it into a property. We have already ascertained that typically property prices on average double every ten years or so. Based on that assumption, after ten years you would expect that £25k to be worth around £50k, wouldn't you?

That would be the case if you had bought a £25k property outright. However, when buying property, you would normally use the £25k as a deposit. And with a £25k deposit, you would be able to get a small property worth £100k as a buy-to-let.

So, your £25k would actually become £125k after ten years (House price has doubled (200%), mortgage is still original (75%) - so equity was 25% is now 125%). That equates to a whopping 40% return on investment every year, just for buying one property.

This is why lots of people who buy property early on in life become wealthy almost by accident after time.

This is just a very basic illustration of what's possible through the acquisition of property and highlighting basic economic history.

"You can't live off equity growth alone."

Owning a property in the knowledge that it will massively go up in value over time and that you will reap the rewards later on in life through equity growth is brilliant. But that alone won't pay you a wage to live off in the meantime.

The really great thing about property investing is that if you know what you are doing, then not only can you benefit massively from equity growth, but you can actually get a wage too through renting out the property as a buy-to-let.

Let's have a look at the numbers.

Average property price: £230,000

Deposit: £57,500

Monthly mortgage repayments £862

Monthly expenses £50

Average monthly rent £960

Monthly profit £48

These are based on today's (July 2020 UK) national averages; house prices are £230k and rents are £959.

A 25% deposit is the normal standard amount to put down for a mortgage.

I use a 6% interest rate, interest-only mortgage; independent mortgage brokers are currently fixing them at 3.18%, but I use 6% as a worst-case scenario.

Approximate monthly expenses are as follows: landlord insurance £180 per year, management costs will depend on if you manage it yourself or use an agent, maintenance costs £35 per month as a ballpark, but again it depends on how you manage the property. Just with these basic average figures, you are achieving a 1% return on investment. That doesn't sound a lot, but when compared to the banks' average of 0.1% it's a lot better. Plus, you are benefiting twice; not only are you benefiting from the equity growth, but it's paying you a small wage at the same time.

Let's look at the numbers of the average bank versus the average property.

AVERAGE PROPERTY

Total investment: £57,500

Annual profit: £576

Return on investment: 1%

Plus: EQUITY GROWTH

AVERAGE BANK

Total investment: £57,500

Annual profit: £57

Return on investment: 0.1%

Minus: DEPRECIATION

TYPES OF PROPERTY

There are many types of property, and all can be great investments depending on what strategy you choose. There's commercial property (offices, warehouses, shops, land, etc.) and residential property (people's homes, buy-to-lets (B2L), serviced accommodation (SA)/AirB&B, houses in multiple occupation (HMOs), and so on).

I believe in writing about what I know. So, I'm not going to try and talk about every type of property and strategy. My focus has been on developing property, such as commercial to residential conversions, and, within that, HMOs, which in my opinion are the holy grail of the buy-to-let market. Let me tell you why.

Houses in multiple occupation (HMOs)

The examples I have outlined so far are all based on national statistics and basically outline how profitable property investing can be.

HMOs are, by far, the best properties to invest in and give the best returns on investment due to their multiple rents, which are much more than a single-occupancy single rent house.

The cost to buy a 3–4 bed single let versus a 3–4 bed multi-let are the same, but whereas for single-let the monthly rent is on average £960 with £50 costs monthly, you can get on average £450 per room, let's say four rooms so £1,800 in rent. The rule of thumb for costs is £100 per room monthly = £400 costs.

Let's look at the numbers for a multi-let compared to a single-let.

SINGLE-LET

Property price: £230,000

Deposit: £57,500

Monthly mortgage repayments: £862

Monthly expenses: £50

Monthly rent: £960

Monthly profit: £40

Return on investment: 1%

Plus: EQUITY GROWTH

MULTI-LET

Property price: £230,000

Deposit: £57,500

Monthly mortgage repayments: £862

Monthly expenses: £400

Monthly rent: £1,800

Monthly profit: £538

Return on investment: 11.2%

Plus: EQUITY GROWTH

So, now I have demonstrated to you how profitable property investing can be, and in particular why HMOs are a great choice. The next thing to consider is what strategies there are that you can use, and which one might be best in a particular situation.

CHAPTER 3

CHOOSING THE RIGHT INVESTMENT STRATEGY

There are lots of different strategies in property investment. In this chapter, I'll look at the main ones and then summarise the pros and cons of each to help you identify when to use them. Later on in chapter 5 I will take you through a couple of case studies from my experience, let's start with my favourite!

BUY, REFURBISH, REFINANCE, & RENT (BRRR)

This is by far my favourite strategy in property investing and is also known as "momentum investing". This is where you buy a property, add value through a renovation or conversion (e.g. a three-bed house to a six-bed HMO), then, once you've owned the property for six months, you can legally re-mortgage it for the uplifted value and usually get most or all your initial investment back to be recycled into the next one. Hence the phrase "momentum investing".

Let's use the above example figures but as a BRRR:

Property price: £230,000

Mortgage: £172,500

Deposit: £57,500

Refurbishment: £80,000

TOTAL INITIAL INVESTMENT: £137,500

Revalued price: £420,000

Re-mortgaged: £315,000

EQUITY IN PROPERTY: 105,000

THE INITIAL INVESTMENT PAID BACK PLUS £5,000

Monthly mortgage repayments: £1,575

Expenses: £600

Monthly rent six-bed: £2,700

MONTHLY PROFIT: £525

RETURN ON INVESTMENT "INFINITE" (INITIAL INVESTMENT BACK)

PLUS: EQUITY GROWTH

Assessing a potential BRRR deal

Many things are needed to assess a potential BRRR HMO deal effectively. The first thing is to know your specific target area and to have researched the rental demand and equity growth there. Then, look for (ideally but not essential) motivated sellers (i.e. if a property is both for sale and for rent, or the listing says cash only sale or no chain, etc.). You can also set your search criteria to view the oldest and most reduced listings to help you look for these, as these will be vendors that are most open for negotiation on terms of sale and who may be more open to selling a bit below market value (BMV), and that may help you structure a creative deal with more options.

Look at the floor plan along with Google Maps aerial and street view to see what potential the property has to extend and add rooms (when doing this, bear in mind the national minimum room sizes – later in this book). Also, look to see if other properties on that street have done any extensions or loft conversions. You can check if they have any roof lights next door; that might indicate they have had a conversion done. This means that, if others on the street have done an extension or conversion, then it's much more likely you will be granted permission to do something similar.

Check if the property is in an Article 4 or conservation area, (article 4 explained on page 85) and, if so, what restrictions they have. Ideally, look for a property where you can use permitted development rights, if possible. Go to the planning portal online and check for any previous planning applications that may have been made on that property or any other properties on that street; this will all help you ascertain feasibility for potential.

So, now you have done all that, you will need to work out some costs for your proposed works. Here are some rough ballpark build/refurb costs to work with (2021 UK-EAST):

Basic Flip: £400 per m2

Mini-Mo: £500 per m2

HMO with en suites: £650 per m2

Commercial to residential: £850 per m2

Loft conversion: £25–35k

Build costs to extend/new build: £1,700 per m2

Next, check the gross development value (GDV). It's best to do this in three different ways, to get an average value.

1. Call a couple of estate agents (preferably agents that you already have a relationship with) to present your idea and ask. Do not ask the agent that the property

is listed with, as they may not have considered its potential and in turn talk to the vendor.

2. Once you know how many square metres your proposed floor area will be, check the Office of National Statistics residential sale price per m2 in that specific area and run the numbers. (shorturl.at/ksPY0)

3. Research RightMove, Zoopla, and on the market sold prices on that street and surrounding streets to see comparable properties to get an average in that area.

Once you have all these numbers, you can work out if it stacks up as a deal. Most bridging companies will want to see at least 20% profit on cost prior to exit. If it's a BRRR, then your exit is refinancing, so the second part is stacking it up as a deal. I would always initially stress test using a 6% mortgage repayment to allow for fluctuation in the market and allow £100 per rentable room for running costs. Make sure you include agents' fees, legal fees, refurb cost, stamp duty, insurance, certificates, letting agents' management fees, plus anything else.

If you get this far and it still stacks up as a deal, start looking for information about the vendor. Ideally, you want to talk to them directly to see why they are selling. Do they live there? Is it tenanted? Do they need the money now? Are they a fed-up landlord to the property? Is there a company registered to that address? If so, who are the directors? Have there been planning applications made for that address? If so, who made the applications? Was it the owner? You can go to Land Registry and pay £3 for the title deeds; that will give you their name and tell you if they have a mortgage on it or not. Once you have their name, you can look them up to see if they are on Facebook, LinkedIn, Instagram, etc. There is a lot of due diligence that can be done on the internet before you even go to view the property. If you do manage to get their details and speak with the vendor directly, but the property is listed with an agent, then it's good practice to be ethical and make it clear that you are not trying to cut out the estate agent and you will pay their fee. Go and view the property and make an offer.

It's important to point out that once you have got this system honed down it should be applied quickly to ascertain if a deal is even a deal.

Beware of "analysis paralysis"! So many people I see and speak to struggle to find/make deals and spend far too much time over-analysing potential deals, wasting their precious time. Everything I have just gone through should be a box-ticking exercise at the beginning. Then, once an agreement is secured between you and the vendor and option agreement/planning is in place etc., it will work even better once analysed on the higher lever in much more detail. After that, who wouldn't want to invest is the question? All that is needed in the beginning is imagination, enthusiasm, and building relationships.

Understanding buildings with 20 years' experience in construction and a massively successful building company behind me, along with two investment properties, I understand what it takes to get a deal together. Before you need to go nuts with all the all-too-important analysis, get it together on the lower level first; just imagination and relationships should be the focus.

RENT TO RENT (R2R)

This is a great strategy if you have limited capital and want to raise funds for deposits to start buying developments of your own. This is where you pay a landlord a fixed guaranteed rent for their property, usually for a three, five, or seven-year term. You inform, agree your intentions, and have a solicitor draw up the agreement; you then rent the property room by room to maximize its rental capability that after costs and rent to the landlord makes you a profit. This strategy delivers exceptional return on investment due to the extremely low initial investment needed.

Initial investment (legal and set up): £4,000

Monthly rent to landlord: £960

Monthly expenses: £400

Monthly rent: £1,800

Monthly profit £440

Return on investment: 132%

The rule of 1.5 for assessing R2Rs

Kevin Mcdonnel talks about the rule of 1.5. It is a simple metric that can be used to assess feasibility for a potential R2R deal, and it works like this.

Let's say you've found a property for rent that has five rooms, and you can get £450 per room per month. To pay yourself first, you multiply the achievable monthly rent for 1.5 rooms, so £450 x 1.5 = £675, then add the monthly expenses to this figure, say £500 (£100 per room approx), so £675 + £450 = £1,175. Then, deduct this amount from the total achievable rent of £2,250 (5 x £450) to give you the maximum amount of £1,075 that you can afford to give the landlord as a guaranteed rent. Every pound you can negotiate under this amount adds to your £675 profit.

Total achievable rent: £2,250 (5 x £450)

Minus: Pay yourself first £675 (1.5 x £450)

Minus: Expenses £500 (5 x 100)

Equals: £1,075 (maximum you can afford to give the landlord)

This rule of 1.5 means that even if you have one empty room you still get 50% profit from one of the four remaining rooms that is rented.

This metric only works with properties from three to six rooms. For a property with six or more rooms, use a profit of £125 per room to pay yourself first.

PURCHASE LEASE OPTIONS (PLO)

This can be an amazing tool to invest in property if you are unable to get a mortgage, and it does not require a large deposit. A purchase lease option (PLO) is an agreement drawn up by solicitors between you and a vendor that gives you the right, but not the obligation, to buy at a fixed price, for a fixed period of time (usually a three, five, or seven-year term) that during that time permits you to use the property in return for a monthly rent. You need to pay a financial consideration to the vendor. This is in return for the option to buy. The option fee can be from just £1 up to £20K. The great thing about PLOs is that the agreement is essentially a blank head of terms that you can write into whatever is agreed between you and the vendor. This means that you can control a property and gain a rental income from it, without the need for the usual 25% deposit or even a mortgage! You can either save up the monthly (lease) rental and use it as a deposit at the end of the term to buy the property or sell the property on for more than the agreed option price, as after five to seven years property prices should have increased, and you keep the difference.

The first important part of this is that the vendor doesn't need money from the sale of the property now. If they are selling the property because they don't want the hassle of it, and they don't need the cash from the sale now, then a PLO would be a great solution. PLOs work best with properties for sale on the open market that have no equity, or are in negative equity, where the mortgage debt is higher than the value of the property.

The second important part is that the owner's mortgage should ideally be a low-interest rate, a buy to let mortgage, an interest only mortgage, a long term left on the mortgage, or no mortgage at all.

You can find these if you look for a property that is listed with an estate agent and a letting agent at the same time. This usually means that the vendor is motivated to sell but is struggling to do so. They are then prepared to rent until they can sell. This is exactly what you are proposing with a PLO. You will pay them a monthly rent until you can buy it at some point in the future. Look for a tired or retiring landlord who no longer wants the hassle of their buy-to-let (BTL) property, who may also be more open to creative solutions than the average motivated seller.

Agreed purchase price (seven-year term): £230,000

Upfront option fee: £5,000

Small refurb: £15,000

Monthly lease fee to landlord: £100

Monthly mortgage: £199

Monthly expenses: £600

Monthly rent: £1,800

Monthly profit: £901

Return on investment: 72%

JOINT VENTURE (JV)

This is another great strategy to raise funds for deposits to start buying developments of your own. You determine that a property has the potential for development and mutually agree with somebody who has funds or a vendor to do a Joint venture (JV), in turn paying them a share of the property's uplifted value. This doesn't have to be a 50/50 split: it can be whatever you agree to be fair, depending on what each party brings to the table.

It is crucially important that you get on very well with your JV partner, and, as a rule of thumb, if you feel comfortable enough to have them stay the night in your home then JV-ing with them should be okay. For this to work with a vendor, they would need to own the property outright or have very little mortgage left on it, and you will need to take the time to build a relationship with them, understanding their needs and ensuring that they are happy to wait to receive more money at a set future date rather than their lesser asking amount a lot sooner. It's important to create a win–win solution for both parties involved, while being careful not to put the idea in their head and then they go and do it for themselves. This can be done by you bringing value – make sure you can bring value to them with a deal. To protect both parties involved, this should be done through solicitors under the umbrella of a "special purchase vehicle" (SPV – see below).

Below is how a special purchase vehicle works between you and a vendor.

SPECIAL PURPOSE VEHICLE (SPV)

An SPV is very straightforward and developers/solicitors have been using them for years.

It's a limited company that exists only to hold a property.

The vendor has the security of full control over the property while it exists.

An SPV states clearly within it who owns the property until an agreed set date for completion of works and release of set agreed funds.

It states clearly within it who is responsible for all bills, management, and caretaking of the property while it exists.

It states clearly within it who is responsible for the renovation works, with a set agreed completion date.

It enables a bridging loan for 100% of the renovation works with no deposit.

Then, with a new higher value, you can re-finance 75% LTV (loan to value) that will enable the pre-agreed amount of funds to be released to the vendor on the set date.

Property is passed to the investor, and the SPV is closed.

An SPV not only protects both parties but also by a vendor putting property or land within an SPV it enables a bridging loan to be taken out that will cover 100% of the works without having to pay a deposit whatsoever. An SPV has the security of the property within it, meaning you would eliminate the extra cost you would normally incur for the borrowing for purchase as well.

Some of this saving can then be passed on to the vendor as an incentive to work with you, as they will receive over the asking price for a property that they may not have seen any potential in or not have had the resources to develop by themselves.

PURCHASE OPTIONS (PO)

Purchase options can be extremely lucrative if done correctly along with the necessary research and due diligence and with very little initial investment needed.

Here's how it works. You look for/find a property, land, or commercial building that fits your criteria for development. You then make an assignable agreement or "purchase option" (PO), drawn up by solicitors between you and the owners, that gives you exclusive rights to purchase the property or land at a pre-agreed price, subject to a successful planning application. You then submit plans and acquire planning permission, thus uplifting the value of the property or land.

At this point, you can then sell on the land with planning permission for the new uplifted value, pay the owner, and pocket the difference, or go on to develop the site yourself to maximise profits. Another string to your bow could be to joint venture (JV) with the owners as if you were to put the land into an SPV company that I talked about earlier. This would enable you to take out bridging finance for 100% of the development with no deposit needed, as the SPV company would have the asset of the land within it as a security against the borrowing. An additional rule of thumb criteria for bridging is to have at least 20% profit on cost (POC) or 70% loan to gross development value (LTGDV) for them to fund your development.

It's important that you take into consideration the vendor's needs; I see so many people fail to get these and PLOs over the line due to trying to push an idea onto a vendor without taking the time to understand the vendor's needs. It's simple – you meet their needs or fix their problem, you will be able to strike a deal, win–win.

The great thing about purchase options (PO) is that

once you have a purchase option in place with planning permission it is an extremely attractive investment for people who potentially want to invest. You have a contract for a fixed amount on the property or land with planning in place so you can also get quotes for the development to accompany your offer to them, so it's clear to see current value cost to develop and gross development value (GDV).you may want to consider multiple exits when approaching people to invest, such as re-finance on a mortgage at the higher value as a multi-let, single-let, holiday-let, or even mixed-use with some commercial, or as a sale as this gives them further security and helps mitigate risk for them.

It's also important to point out that quite a lot of background research is required in the specific location where you want to search for property or land, to increase your chances of success.

Most local councils have an online interactive map where you can search a location for previous and current planning applications. This is really useful; when looking, if you find an application has been rejected or lapsed for time, it doesn't mean that it will never get planning permission. In more cases than not, a small tweak to plans can mean the difference between planning being granted or not. This is usually through the incompetence of an architect's or homeowner's planning submission or poor communication with the local council, and, for this reason, I strongly recommend getting in touch and building a relationship with a really good planning consultant, preferably one accredited to the RTPI (Royal Town Planning Institute) to help you with advice in your search and also to completely take care of your submissions for a fixed price.

Also, it's a great idea to read through the "local plan" as well that is published by the local council. This is where they allocate areas for residential or commercial development (also available on the interactive maps). Also, read the national planning policy framework so that you have a really good understanding of the location where you want to do development. It will make you more efficient in being able to rule out areas within your location and save you time. Obviously, in the beginning, it takes time to learn all this, but you will find that you will get better and better at it the more you do it. Practice makes perfect, as they say.

So, let's say you have done all that, and you have found a plot that ticks your criteria. Now, go to the Land Registry website; again, they have an interactive map search option that is really good. Pay £3 for the title deed that has the owner's details and get in touch with them. Again, I talk about how to search for details on an owner earlier on in the book and the same applies here. I recommend writing a simple letter to them to get in touch with you and start negotiations.

Lastly, the important thing here is to be laser-focused. First, concentrate on finding a site that will potentially work. Second, get an agreement with the owner. Third, get the planning done. Fourth, approach people who may potentially invest. Of course, it's preferable to already have money in place to do this, or a person who has given you a commitment, but you will find as you get more seasoned in developing if a deal's good the money will always follow; I should know, I am a testament to that actually happening, so have faith and good luck.

DON'T WASTE TIME

Doing research with maximum efficiency, I recommend as always to pick one strategy and one location and focus on it (F-O-C-U-S – follow one course until successful). It's easy to get distracted and waste time. I find the best way is to time yourself with 50-minute intervals when doing research; 50 minutes seems to work best with concentration. Do 50 minutes, then take a 5-minute break, and if you feel you can do another stint then do another 50 minutes fully submersed to be super-efficient in your search. Hope this helps.

SUMMARY

Let's look back at those strategies and see the benefits and drawbacks of each.

VEHICLE	PROS	CONS/RISKS
BRRR (HMO)	• Rapid turnover of funds • Fast appreciation of equity • Own the property once complete • Great ROI	• Revaluation being less than anticipated • Use a good builder to ensure the renovation doesn't overrun
R2R (HMO)	• Good for limited capital • Fast cashflow • Exceptional ROI	• Don't own the property • No equity growth
PLO	• Good for limited capital • Fast cashflow • No mortgage needed • Great ROI • Option to buy with accumulated profit as deposit	• Takes time to find and build rapport with a landlord open to the idea • Need to bring value to the table • Need a robust agreement
JV/SPV	• No funds needed	• Must get on with partner • Need to bring value to the table • Need a robust agreement
PO	• Little initial investment • Extremely profitable • Fast appreciation of equity	• Takes time to find and build rapport with a landlord open to the idea • Use a good planning consultant to increase your chances of success • Need a robust agreement

* * *

I know that was a lot of information to take in so far! And I'm afraid there's still more to come in the next chapter. This time, we need to think about how to measure your success. Having a consistent way of tracking performance is vitally important – both to help you decide what type of investment strategy you want to use and to know how successful you are at using it.

CHAPTER 4

METRICS FOR
MEASURING SUCCESS

There are three major ways of measuring the performance of an investment: return on investment (ROI), return on equity (ROE), and yield. I'll look at these in turn. After that, I want to talk about a couple of other considerations/side-notes that are good rules of thumb to keep in mind when investing – or indeed any business and looking after your money in general. This first one, ROI, is THE most important metric to use. Once you know what ROI you want to achieve for your money, you can then decide whether to enter an investment or not based on the personal ROI criteria you have set yourself.

RETURN ON INVESTMENT (ROI)

ROI is a metric used to describe how an investment performs. It is one of the simplest, most important ways to compare investments and it is used across all investment vehicles, not just property. ROI is the percentage of your total investment that you can expect to receive in a year.

So, for example, if you've invested £10k at 5%, you will receive 5% of your investment in one year; that means 5% of £10k = £500 each year until you receive all of your initial investment back. There is also a direct correlation in terms of time to get back all your initial investment using this method too.

The basic formula is:

Annual profit ÷ initial investment x 100 = ROI%Time correlation to get your initial investment back simplified is:

25% = 4 years, 50% = 2 years, 100% = 1 year, 200% = 6 months, etc.

ROI you should expect to receive through various property strategies:

Single buy-to-let (BTL): 7% +

HMO buy-to-let (BTL): 15% +

Purchase lease Option (PLO): 50% +

Rent-to-rent (R2R): 100% +

*These figures come from
https://propertyinvestorsnetwork.co.uk/
how-to-calculate-return-on-investment/

RETURN ON EQUITY (ROE)

ROE is also a metric used to describe how an investment performs. It can be used on an individual property or across an entire portfolio.

For example, you own a house that is worth £230k with £100k of equity; the mortgage payments are £500 monthly, and you receive £700 rent from a tenant. £700 - £500 x 12 months = £2,400 income annually. Divide that by the £100k of equity x 100 = 24%. This is the percentage return on equity you are getting on your money that is tied up in that house.

The basic formula is:

Net income ÷ equity x 100 = ROE

YIELD

Yield is another metric used to describe how an investment performs (predominately used by estate agents). Crucially, though, this doesn't take into account any costs as a property owner (e.g. management fees, void periods, maintenance repair bills, insurances, taxes, etc.). More crucially, it doesn't take into account your initial investment either. I would, therefore, recommend NOT to use this as a metric. This is how it works.

For example, if a Property is £100k and the total annual gross rent is £10k, the yield will be 10%.

The basic formula is:

Annual gross rent ÷ Value of property = YIELD

THE LAWS OF ACCUMULATING WEALTH

For me, ROI is the most important metric to use, but alongside that there are some very basic finance rules to follow, set out 8,000 years ago in ancient Babylon and written about by George S Clason in his book "The Richest Man In Babylon", that still apply today. Like the laws of gravity, these laws apply for the accumulation of wealth, and they are as follows …

The seven cures for a lean purse …

1. Start thy purse to fattening.

2. Control thy expenditures.

3. Make thy gold multiply.

4. Guard thy treasures from loss.

5. Make of thy dwelling a profitable investment.

6. Insure a future income.

7. Increase thy ability to earn.

Aside from these seven cures for a lean purse, he also wrote about the five rules of gold:

1. Gold cometh gladly and in increasing quantity to any man who will put by not less than one-tenth of his earnings to create an estate for his future and that of his family.

2. Gold laboreth diligently and contentedly for the wise owner who finds for its profitable employment, multiplying even as the flocks of the field.

3. Gold clingeth to the protection of the cautious owner who invests it under the advice of men wise in its handling.

4. Gold slippeth away from the man who invests it in businesses or purposes with which he is not familiar, or which are not approved by those skilled in its keep.

5.   Gold flees the man who would force it to impossible earnings or who followeth the alluring advice of tricksters and schemers or who trusts it to his own inexperience and romantic desires in investment.

Translated into today's world, for me, the main points to take from all of these is that when investing in property, or any business for that matter, you should always apply the following:

1.   Save at least 10% of everything you earn.
2.   Invest that 10% saved and invest the proceeds of your investments in new investments.
3.   Only invest in things that you have knowledge in.
4.   Work hard to improve your earning capability.

* * *

Okay, so we've covered how property investing works and established how profitable it can be, along with the main strategies and metrics to track/set performance. In the next chapter, I'm going to change gear and talk about my own experiences, which I've divided up into a couple of "case studies" for you. Enjoy!

CHAPTER 5

CASE STUDIES FROM MY EXPERIENCE

CASE STUDY 1: (R2R) THREE-BED MINI-MO

For me, the whole point of getting into property from the get-go was to get out of debt and to be financially independent so I could choose when, and if, I wanted to work. So, if I was going to have a passive income from property, it needed to be exactly that, passive! One of first things I did while networking was to find a great local letting agent who specialized in HMOs to manage my properties and deal with all of the day-to-day management, tenant finding, maintenance, etc.

It was also important to me to invest locally to utilize

my most valuable asset, my building company, Propertyfix Builders Ltd, so I chose my target area to be in the city 30 mins from home, close to the city centre where there is strong rental demand and good capital growth.

I figured a good start for me would be to do a rent-to-rent in the beginning to move forward as a property investor. This would help raise capital for deposits and raise my profile as a property investor at the same time. So, with that in mind, I quickly set about to secure my first rent-to-rent investment property. It was a Victorian terrace three-bed mini-mo. I sourced this through an advert I posted on Facebook and arranged a meeting with the owner. We agreed a fixed guaranteed rent on a three-year contract, and I explained my intentions. We signed contracts, and I gave it a small refurb using my building company. Then I rented the three rooms separately through an agent. After the rent to the landlord and costs, I made a monthly profit of £275 with a total setup cost of £4k.

A good tip is to look for the terraced houses that have an alley next to them. I identified that by utilizing the alley for quick, easy access, using the back door as the main entrance, would enable me to use the front room as an extra bedroom, and with four rooms upstairs we offered one smaller room included with each double bedroom as a free extra, and this is exactly what I did.

Let's have a look at the numbers …

Investment property 1 (Rent-to-Rent R2R)

Refurb and contract: £4,000

Rent to landlord: £750

Monthly costs: £600

Monthly rent: £1,625

Monthly profit: £275

Return on investment: 82.5%

With my first R2R investment deal in the bag, I was on a run and didn't want to lose traction, so I continued to look for more deals as the first one had just given me a massive boost.

Key takeaways

- Utilise what skills you already have
- Find a good local letting agent
- Look for creative ways to maximise bedrooms

CASE STUDY 2: (BRRR) SHOP AND TWO FLATS TO SIX-BED HMO

While at a study class learning about strategies, all the students and I were set a challenge by the host that, while on lunch break, we were to contact an estate agent that we hadn't spoken to before. So, I did, and I found that a property that I had seen three months prior had come back on the market at an online auction. It was a shop with two flats, bang in the centre of my specific target area. It had previously sold at auction for 360k and was now back on the market with a starting bid of just 250k. it was obvious to me straight away with all my building experience that there was great potential to convert it into a six-bed HMO. I did some research online to find its current value and gross development value (GDV) as well as speaking to my estate agent. I ran the numbers and it stacked up. The sellers were obviously motivated, as I had learned that the previous two sales had fallen through recently due to both buyers pulling out for personal reasons. I didn't want to miss out on it and given it had previously sold for 360k I wanted to make sure my bid was accepted. So, I stuck my neck out and with no money or investor on board placed a bid for 280k, and within 24 hours it was accepted. Whoo-hoo, I was elated, but literally had no money to even pay the 6k deposit needed to secure it. As far as I was concerned, this was meant to be and would be mine no matter what. So, I stalled them for another 14 days while I found a way to borrow the money and eventually managed to borrow it.

Then, out of nowhere, the first COVID-19 lockdown hit, along with all the uncertainty, but I saw this as an opportunity to ask if they would accept 10k less than my original offer due to all the uncertainty, and to cover me before I paid the 6k deposit that I had borrowed. They got back to me by the end of the day with a yes, so I paid the deposit and secured the property for a purchase price of 270k.

I now needed to get plans drawn up and submit a pre-planning application to ascertain if my idea would be accepted by the council. I had done my homework and knew that it wasn't in a conservation area and there was no Article 4 in place either. I also knew that we could do a loft conversion for the extra bedrooms under permitted development rights, and it was clear to see that next door had done one, as there were roof lights visible from the road. The change of use for the shop from A1 to C3 (residential) was the only potential stumbling block; after that, the loft and the C3–C4 (single occupancy residential to small HMO) change of use would all be under permitted development rights too. (planning classifications can be found here: https://www. planningportal.co.uk/ info/200130/common_projects/9/ change_of_use). I would still need to get full planning later on to adapt the two shopfront windows, but I was sure this would be acceptable based on a conversation with the local council planning case manager, plus similar properties in the area had had similar changes. I wouldn't need full planning permission to be a large HMO as it would only be six beds, so only a license would be required. The shop hadn't been used as a shop since the 1980s, and there had been all sorts of building works on the same street that were not in keeping with the rest of the street, so I was confident a change of use to residential would be acceptable.

I desperately needed to find more funds, so I set about speaking to everybody I knew as well as people I didn't. I went all out networking and spoke to at least seven or eight new potential investors per day, and, after a few weeks of doing that, I finally managed to borrow 10k from a new investor and now friend that I had met at a property class. 10k would just about cover the costs I needed for the plans and the pre-app to be submitted, which was great – so far, so good!

Then, the pre-app came back, and as I had predicted

indicated that change of use to residential would be acceptable, although I would still have to apply for full planning if I wanted to proceed; that was fine. This was great news. Next, I approached bridging companies to help raise funds. Their criteria are at least 20% profit on cost (POC), and I knew that I had around 30% so that would be okay. They offered to loan 65% of the purchase price and 100% of the build cost based on the numbers I gave them, and they gave me a list of approved RICS surveyors to get a valuation done before they would commit. I did that, and the valuation came back with a current value of £250k and a GDV of £575k, just as I had predicted.

Now that I had a commitment from the bridging company, all I needed was the deposit money of £130k to enable them to bridge it. I had done my numbers and knew the maximum I could offer to an investor for an 8- to 12-month loan. I knew I needed two months for planning, plus three months to build, then refinance, which can take up to three months, and pull all the money out to pay the investor in time.

I took the time to put together a glossy investor pack that presented the opportunity well, to then pitch to potential investors and to everyone I knew too. But being in the middle of COVID-19 lockdown it proved a lot harder, as this meant all networking had gone virtual and people were very nervous due to all the uncertainty, not wanting to invest. This proved to be extremely challenging; however, I'm no quitter.

I had a brain wave. What if the vendor was willing to wait for the money but receive more than the agreed price later on? This way, I could present a joint venture (JV) to him within an SPV. This would eliminate the cost of the borrowing for the purchase price and would mean a bridging loan was possible with no deposit. I could then pass on some of the saving to him as an incentive of around 10k more than the agreed purchase price, and it would be win–win for both of us. I had already got the vendor's mobile telephone number from the agent who showed us around, so I started an email campaign to test the water with him, asserting that nobody was lending due to the COVID-19 lockdown uncertainty.

After a few weeks of emails, it became clear that they didn't want to wait any longer as they had already previously been messed about, and they just wanted the money with no ties. We should have already completed by now anyway, so I didn't want to push my luck any further.

Then, right on cue, one of the people that I had previously sent an investor pack to got back to me with an offer of a loan from his finance company for £80k. this was great, but

I was still short £40k.

Throughout all this, I had been keeping in touch with my investor friend who had originally loaned me the initial £10k. We had been speaking every other day and had become fairly close. He had been taking a great interest in this deal and had seen how hard I was working to make it happen. He didn't have any building experience and was keen to learn from me, and out of nowhere he turned round and pledged the final £40k that was needed. This was on the basis that while he was getting a fixed return on his money, he could earn and learn while he invested and get to understand orchestrating a renovation, conversion, and actively being part of the process to gain experience for himself. That was fine by me, as we had become close and we got on well and were in line with each other's core values. I had now raised all the funds needed and was set.

With all the deposit needed in place, I went back to the vendor with two offers, which were: A) I could pay £250k now and it would only take about 6–8 weeks to complete, or B) I could pay him £280k in 8 months as a Joint venture (JV), as I had previously proposed.

He quickly decided that the £250k was preferable to him. This meant that last minute I had successfully negotiated an extra £20k, making a total of £30k of my original offer of £280k for a property that had sold three months ago for £360k. I was elated.

I went back to my architect and instructed him to draw up the full plans. He did these and submitted them in three sets, so if there was an issue with one part of the planning, then we would only need to resubmit one part and not have to submit the whole thing again. He did one for the change of use, one for the bay windows, and one for the loft together with the C3-C4 change of use from single dwelling house to house in multiple occupation under permitted development, submitting each one staggered to the council.

I also brought in my interior designer at this stage to work alongside my architect, as a designer will help design a layout based on user experience. They will also consider furniture layout, lighting etc., so essentially starting from the end and working back. That seems to make so much sense to me, as an architect will usually just try to maximize the number of rooms and miss end-user feel. It's far better to have fewer rooms with higher rent and fewer voids than more rooms for less rent and more voids.

For me, it's all about creating super high-end co-living spaces where I would want to live and creating a better standard of living within the market. I love renovating buildings, so it's important to me that my heart's in it. Obviously, in the beginning, when analysing a property deal, it's about the numbers and if it stacks, but after that, it's all about the love and creativeness for me. And on the plus side, statistically, consumer-focused businesses will always super-succeed other businesses no matter what the markets are doing.

Now I needed to organize the building work, and as I didn't have time to submit full building control construction notes, I would need to apply for building under what's called a "building notice". This is a simple application form to be able to start works upon full planning permission within 48 hours of approval. So, I contacted the local building control officer to confirm what I would need under the notice. This was 1) an independent structural engineer's report and 2) a fire safety report. As long as I could produce these items upon request to them, so that they would be able to come out at the relevant intervals to inspect the works, we were set to start.

Lastly, to be thorough, I contacted the local private housing sector department and applied for an HMO license, so that I could run all this past them to make sure we could start works with everyone being on the same page.

I then used my building company, Propertyfix Builders Ltd, to carry out the works that were completed on time and budget, and while works were underway, I organised my letting agent to do a virtual tour to start marketing it before the end, to be super-efficient.

It was now time to get a revaluation, and I had ended up well exceeding the original projected gross development value (GDV) of £575k to £650k- £675k due to going above and beyond the extra mile on all accounts, especially with the end finish.

When refinancing, I highly recommend putting together an info pack or property overview of about 3–4 pages to demonstrate to the valuer how you have achieved the new (GDV) value. This should include before and after pictures and floor plans, schedule of works, compatibles, local agents' valuations, and anything else that reinforces your case for the price you believe it to now be worth.

Refinancing pays back all the bridging, and my investor friend with left NO MONEY LEFT IN the property, and I now had £168,750k of equity in a property that would not only pay all its own bills but pay me £1,162.50 on top passively per month forever, plus with the added benefit of capital growth over time. All that's needed now is to NOT sell the property, and every 10–12 years the equity will have doubled and continue to do so as long as I hold it.

Here are the numbers …

Property price: £250,000

Fees and costs: £18,000

Refurbishment: £179,000

Finance – bridging costs: £59,000

Total initial investment: £506,000

Revalue price: £675,000

Re-mortgage: £506,250

EQUITY IN PROPERTY: £168,750

NO MONEY LEFT IN

Monthly mortgage: £1,687

Monthly costs: £1,200

Monthly rent six-bed: £4,050

MONTHLY PROFIT: £1,162.50

PLUS: EQUITY GROWTH

Key takeaways

- Look for "motivated sellers"
- Change of use can be lucrative
- Make a professional prospectus to attract investors

- Need to be creative to raise finance
- Design with the end-user focus
- Think ahead with planners and council
- Make a valuation pack to maximise valuation

EXTRA CASE STUDY:
(PRIVATE INVESTOR, INVEST AND LEARN)

A fellow property investor friend I met through networking invested in my above BRRR case study 2. We mutually agreed on terms and crucially were both in line with each other's core values, both bringing something to the table creating a win–win scenario. I had extensive experience in refurbs, and he had capital and wanted to learn from me. I had contracts drawn up and signed by both parties. Good communication is essential, and I continuously updated him every step of the way, working closely together throughout the project on every last detail, plus sharing my extensive knowledge of refurbishments and investments.

Side note: terms can be completely flexible and bespoke to meet individual projects and people's needs.

Here's what was agreed …

Loan amount: £50K

Repayment: the full amount of £50k plus interest paid upon refinancing.

Agreements are completely bespoke to meet individual projects/requirements

* * *

Well, that's pretty much most of the essential ingredients needed to start and be successful in property investing, although in my opinion there is one more key ingredient that quite possibly glues all these together that I want to share with you. Before we finish, I want to take a minute to pass on some of my learnings on what you need as a person to be a successful property investor. I make no apologies for this next "far-out" or "woo-woo" chapter. I believe it's essential for you to go into this with your eyes open to what it takes mentally. I certainly wish someone had told *me* before I started!

CHAPTER 6

MINDSET IS VITAL

MINDSET

A good mindset is really important and absolutely key. Property investing is a high-stress environment with lots of big decisions that can be extremely stressful if you don't have the correct mindset to deal with it, and, in my opinion, this is the missing link between failure and success. After reading about my journey, it may well seem to you like an impossibly complex task far out of reach, or it may seem to you that I must have had a few lucky breaks. Truth is, these are the kind of stories we tell ourselves as our minds like to play tricks on us. These are limiting beliefs and cause procrastination or "analysis paralysis". This is when you talk yourself out of doing something based on your current self and not your future self (talked about by Benjamin Hardy in his book). It's important to understand that we are not our thoughts or emotions, and thoughts/emotions are just that, thoughts/emotions, not reality. Fear, for example, most of the time is just that, fear – a thought or emotion, and most of the time the things we fear will happen never even come to fruition. Fear is just one of the emotions hard-wired into us from caveman times to keep us safe from lions and tigers, but today there are no lions or tigers, and half the time we are making decisions using this ancient, out of date emotional programming, being emotionally un-intelligent. We all tend to let our thoughts dictate our reality from pre-conceived notions based on previous experiences that most of the time aren't correct and won't happen. This is why it's important to have awareness and be emotionally intelligent. Big (educated) risks yield big rewards, and thoughts become things, so if you focus on something hard enough (good or bad) you will make it happen. An example of this is if you recollect all the times you have made up your mind on a relationship, or that you need a new car or whatever it might be, and then focused on that thing so much that you made it happen. You made it your new reality, you broke off the relationship or bought that new car. That said, to want something too much can be detrimental and can push that something you want away; for example, going to a tender for a new work contract or job interview or whatever, absolutely desperate to get it, would likely be portrayed by your body language and the words that you use, limiting your chances. But going while in a calm place is more likely to demonstrate your natural glow, increasing your chances of winning the contract or getting the job. The trick is to be in a place of abundance rather than a place of scarcity; the less you push hard for something while in a place of scarcity, and the more you push hard while in a place of abundance, the easier that thing will come to you. For example, recollect a time you lost something that after searching and searching for it, once you finally stopped searching it appeared when you weren't looking. Obviously, there are boundaries to this. I'm not suggesting to flat-out stop wanting or pushing for things, but to come from a place of having, as opposed to wanting; a place of abundance, not scarcity. Sanjay Shah teaches emotional intelligence and that "wants" can usually be rooted back to three core emotions: control, security, and approval. Once you ascertain which is the want you are experiencing, you can begin to accept that want and let it go. To move forward, though, to where you want to be, you will still need to follow whatever the key tasks are required to get there from an educated standpoint, and so long as you follow those tasks set, then you will get to where it is you are aiming to be and achieve your goal. Enjoy the journey in the knowledge that you are heading towards your desired place or future self. These are all key factors to grasp that will help you get ahead more than most, so long as you have a good knowledge base and focus. Dr. Benjamin Hardy has two amazing books, "Personality Isn't Permanent" and "Who Not How", which I encourage you to read.

It is important to understand and adopt all of these attributes and to follow one course until successful, not deviating from it. Be specific, laser-focused. Be decisive with decisions; you must know exactly where and who you aim to be in the future so that you can plan your way there. Without these all-important specifics, thoughts are just fantasies. I find that to make things real they must be written down. Writing them down instantly makes them real; a goal without a plan is just a dream. Never stop learning and mastering your mind; to think you know everything stops you from learning. A place of "I don't know" is best and to hear everything as if for the first time. Get out of your comfort zone, get out of your own way!

Environment is also a major contributing factor that affects mindset, along with negative addiction. The first step is awareness and acceptance of these. If you have a negative addiction, look to replace it with a positive one, and the same for environment. This could be friends, family, or a partner, that perhaps have more of a fixed mindset. If they are not prepared to give you the supportive environment you require to nurture you to move forward, then look to discuss it with them and if necessary, change it. Tony Robins says we are 50% of the five people you spend the most time with. That makes a lot of sense to me.I truly believe that, although these all seem like common knowledge, very few people actually implement these in their lives. They are not a simple "quick fix/buy once"; they need constant daily work and nurturing to reap rewards. Give yourself gratitude hourly, and if you do all these, you will see big results not just in yourself but in the way those around you act towards you too.

MY MISSION

I wrote this book in order to help as many people as I can. I realise that there is another way to live other than just getting up and going to work, day in day out, and never seeming to get ahead. Living beyond your means on unsustainable bad credit. I understand that there is another way, an emotionally educated way, and a financially educated way, through property investing. Money is not everything, and it won't make you happy; you need to be happy first. But money will amplify who you are and its integrity and can certainly give you more of the only limited commodity in life you have – time. Property investing is not for everybody and does require a lot of initial work, but at the end of the day, you get out what you put in, and nobody is going to help you but you! So, what are you waiting for? Take action, seize the opportunity and live life your way.

CHAPTER 7

YOUR NEXT STEPS

So now it's over to you. Here are some resources to help you along the way – films, books, a little philosophy, and ways to reach out to me if you want. I wish you all the very best on your journey!

MEDIA I RECOMMEND

Capital in the 21st Century (documentary)

The Big Short (movie)

Inside Job (documentary)

BOOKS I RECOMMEND

Rich Dad, Poor Dad (Robert Kiyosaki)

Think & Grow Rich (Napoleon Hill)

The Richest Man in Babylon (George S Clason)

Property Magic (Simon Zutshi)

Buy Low, Rent High (Samuel Leeds)

Rent to Rent (Jacquie Edwards)

No Money Down Property Investing (Kevin McDonnell)

Personality Isn't Permanent (Benjamin Hardy)

Who Not How (Benjamin Hardy)

Never Split the difference (Chris Voss)

How to Attract Armchair Investors (Tim Macham)

Eat That Frog (Brain Tracy)

MANTRAS TO LIVE BY

Success is waiting for you just outside your comfort zone

Live in a place of abundance NOT scarcity

Hear everything for the first time! ("I don't know" NOT "I know")

Under-promise and over-deliver

Work "on" your business NOT "in" your business

L-U-C-K: Labouring Under Correct Knowledge

F-O-C-U-S: "Follow one course until successful"

F-E-A-R: "false expectations appearing real"

"A goal without a plan is just a dream!"

"If you always do what you have always done, then you always get what you always got"

"If you say you can, you can, if you say you can't, you can't"

"Work smarter, not harder"

"You don't know what you don't know"

"Nobody is going to help you but you"

"You don't ask, you don't get"

"You give good, you get good"

"It happened for me! Not to me!"

"If you feel like you are surrounded by shit, change your perspective; shit is a fertiliser (hardship creates growth)"

"Your network is your net-worth"

"What other people think of me is none of my business"

"What you say to yourself when you are by yourself" (give yourself gratitude hourly)

"How can I afford it?" NOT "I can't afford it"

"Who can help me achieve my objective?" NOT "how can I achieve my objective?"

You are 50% of the 5 people you spend the most time with

GET IN TOUCH

"Don't wait to get into property",

"get into property and wait!"

Let's start a conversation!

Claim your FREE 30-MIN telephone

consultation with Sebastian

Use voucher code: BUILDINVEST1

In the Contact Us form with a brief message to reserve

your slot at NO COST completely FREE here:

WWW.SEBASTIANMACFARLANE.CO.UK

Other ways to get in touch:

SEB@SEBASTIANMACFARLANE.CO.UK

HTTPS://WWW.FACEBOOK.COM/INVESTORSLTD/

WWW.LINKEDIN.COM/IN/PROPERTYFIX-INVESTORS-LTD

WWW.SEBASTIANMACFARLANE.CO.UK

RULES AND REGULATIONS

There are many legal aspects to property investing – not least protecting the rights of your tenants. I'm not going to try and give you an exhaustive list of all these, as there are many excellent resources online. I've given you pointers to some I've found helpful, along with a few tips of my own.

GOLDEN RULES

Like anything, you must have some parameters to follow when investing in property to ensure you minimize any risk. Simon Zutshi talks about 5 golden rules that I think are extremely important to follow

Always:

- Buy from motivated sellers and below market value
- Buy in an area with strong rental demand
- Buy and hold the property
- Make sure your rent is more than your costs
- Have a cash buffer for unexpected expenses

HMO LAW UK

You are allowed up to four people as a multi-let before the council classes it as an HMO; after that, for five or more people you will need a license. If over six people, you will need a license and full planning. Always check with your local authority, as they vary. You will also need to make sure that you have the correct buy-to-let mortgage product for a multi-let/HMO.

Room sizes HMOs

Below are the national standards (July 2020)

- You will need to check with the local council for your specific area, as they do vary.
- Floor area of any room in the HMO used as sleeping accommodation by one person aged over 10 years is not less than 6.51 square meters.
- Floor area of any room in the HMO used as sleeping accommodation by two persons aged over 10 years is not less than 10.22 square meters.
- Floor area of any room in the HMO used as sleeping accommodation by one person aged under 10 years is not less than 4.64 square meters.

- Any room in the HMO with a floor area of less than 4.64 square meters is not used as sleeping accommodation.

- Any room in the HMO with vaulted (sloping) ceilings, the floor area is only counted from where the ceiling slope is 1.5 meters up from the floor.

For a detailed consideration of the issues in HMO investing in the UK, visit https://www.gov.uk/renting-out-a-property/houses-in-multiple-occupation-hmo

PERMITTED DEVELOPMENTS

When looking for BRRR and commercial-to-residential projects, it's preferable to utilise the permitted development rights for change of use that can be found on the planning portal.

By using these, they will enable you to raise finance offering much more certainty and dramatically reducing risk for potential investors, along with simplifying the planning process.

For a detailed consideration of permitted development rights in the UK, visit:

https://www.planningportal.co.uk/info/200130/common_projects/9/change_of_use/2

ARTICLE 4 DIRECTION

An article 4 direction is made by the local planning authority. It restricts the scope of permitted development rights either in relation to a particular area or site, or a particular type of development anywhere in the authority's area. Its always best to read the actual article 4 direction in your specific location as they vary, there may be an article 4 direction in place but it may not have a restriction on HMOs for example within it.

For a detailed consideration of article 4 direction visit your local council website

TAX

Capital gains tax is one of the significant considerations when managing a property portfolio. It is payable on the increase in value of any property when you sell it.

But if you never sell your property, you never pay capital gains tax. When you die, capital gains tax liability on your property portfolio is dissolved. So, if you constantly re-mortgage your property and recycle the equity into other property investments, you will be increasing your level of debt which at the same time will reduce your net assets and so reduce any inheritance tax liability on your portfolio.

The other important thing you need to understand is which

of your costs you can offset against your tax bill. The largest of these – mortgage payments – has changed several times in the UK in the last few years. There are also rules for professional fees, refurb costs, etc.

For a detailed consideration of the tax issues in property investing in the UK, visit: https://www.gov.uk/renting-out-a-property/paying-tax

ABOUT THE AUTHOR

Sebastian Macfarlane has 20 years of extensive experience with complete house renovations, barn conversions, and extensions. Founder of **Propertyfix Builders Ltd**, along with investment company **Propertyfix Investors Ltd**. He is also a graduate of **Simon Zutshi's Property Mastermind 12-month programme** and part of the **property investors network**. He is actively investing in property himself and has a talent of being able to spot/identify potential development projects while having the ability to add real value to them with his building company. His preferred strategy is commercial-to-residential buy, renovate, refinance, and rent (BRRR) co-living HMOs (houses in multiple occupation).

Printed in Great Britain
by Amazon